I0160065

SCREEN PLAY

A R Gurney

BROADWAY PLAY PUBLISHING INC
New York
www.broadwayplaypub.com
info@broadwayplaypub.com

SCREEN PLAY

© Copyright 2005 A R Gurney

All rights reserved. This work is fully protected under the copyright laws of the United States of America.

No part of this publication may be photocopied, reproduced, stored in a retrieval system, or transmitted, in any form or by any means, electronic, mechanical, recording, or otherwise, without the prior permission of the publisher. Additional copies of this play are available from the publisher.

Written permission is required for live performance of any sort. This includes readings, cuttings, scenes, and excerpts. For amateur and stock performances, please contact Broadway Play Publishing Inc. For all other rights please contact W M E.

Cover art by David Prittie

First printing: June 2005
This edition: January 2019
I S B N: 978-0-88145-272-3

Book design: Marie Donovan
Page make-up: Adobe InDesign
Typeface: Palatino
Printed and bound in the U S A

SCREEN PLAY was first produced at the Flea Theater in New York City (Jim Simpson, Artistic Director; Carol Ostrow, Producing Director; Todd Rosen, Managing Director). The play opened on 5 June 2005, with the following cast and creative contributors:

MYRNA .... Raushanah Simmons
NICK.. Drew Hildebrand
SALLY.. Meredith Holzman
WALTER... Brian Morvant
CHARLEY .... Derrick Edwards
SECRETARY PATCH... John Fico
other roles... Kevin T Moore

Director .... Jim Simpson
Assistant director.. Deborah Wolfson
Stage manager.. Lauren Levitt
Costumes.. Melissa Schlachtmeyer
Lighting... Joe Novak
Music director.. Kris Kukul

CHARACTERS & SETTING

MYRNA, *African-American; singer and piano player*
NICK, *owner of Nick's Bar in Buffalo, NY*
SALLY, *attractive wife of…*
WALTER WELLMAN, *distinguished political pundit and activist*
CHARLEY WASHINGTON, *African-American; Chief of Buffalo Police*
SECRETARY ABNER PATCH, *Southern, Deputy Secretary of Homeland Security*
SWING ACTOR, *to play other roles*

The play is designed to be read aloud by the actors at music stands, with stools to sit on behind. They stand when they participate in a scene, sit when they don't. There is no need for props. Costuming should be equally minimal: the actors might dress as if they were auditioning for their parts.

Narrative passages are divided among various actors who should deliver them without playing their main character.

It helps if the actors are familiar with their lines, and if they could synchronize as much as possible the turning of their pages. In other words, while this is a reading it should have a rehearsed quality.

The play takes place approximately fifteen years into the future.

to the Flea Theater
long may it wave

(At rise)

(The actors enter informally and take their places at their music stands. Their positions from stage right to stage left are: MYRNA, SWING ACTOR, SECRETARY PATCH, WALTER, NICK, SALLY, *and* CHARLEY)

MYRNA: *(To audience, before she takes her place)* This is the screenplay of a movie that was deemed too dangerous to produce. So we're doing it as a reading instead.

WALTER: *(To audience)* We begin with significant-sounding music...

OTHER ACTORS: Da-dum.

WALTER: ...and show a globe of the world spinning slowly in space. It stops at a map of the United States as a Voice Over begins.

SECRETARY PATCH: *(To audience: sonorously, as in a movie voiceover)* Not long into the twenty-first century, American power began to wane significantly as she wasted her youth and her treasure on brutal and unnecessary battles abroad. At the same time, much of American life degenerated into hectic celebrations of property and possessions, saturated with pervasive advertising and underscored by an especially self-righteous brand of the Christian religion. As a result, large numbers of Americans began to seek a different life beyond their own borders.

NICK: *(To audience)* Air travel at that time was both uncomfortable and dangerous, so most of this exodus took place by land and sea, and the traditional ports of entry which once welcomed immigrants into the United States now became places of departure for citizens reluctantly ready to bid their country goodbye.

WALTER: *(To audience)* Now on that map we see a number of arrows stretching towards various seaports on the East and West Coasts of the United States, and along its borders with Mexico and Canada.

SECRETARY PATCH: *(To audience)* In response to this exodus...

(Other actors hum quietly a low note.)

SECRETARY PATCH: ...the American government, like most governments aware of their own vulnerability, made it more difficult for its citizens to leave. Passports were cancelled or curtailed, and the nation's lengthy borders carefully patrolled to inhibit those going out as much as those coming in. Yet many Americans still gathered at various departure points, yearning for a more sustaining way of life.

WALTER: *(To audience)* We zoom in on one of the arrows on that map…

(More humming)

WALTER: …as it cuts through Washington and Philadelphia and stretches toward Buffalo at the eastern end of Lake Erie…

SECRETARY PATCH: *(To audience)* One of the more popular gathering places was the ancient city of Buffalo, once a thriving port at the end of the Erie Canal and gateway to the developing western states. Its proximity to Canada, which lay just across the turbulent waters of the Niagara River, gave this city a new appeal.

WALTER: *(To audience)* We fade from the map to the call-letters of the local television station W B U F. A newscaster sits at her console reading a bulletin.

SALLY: *(To audience)* This just in…

(SECRETARY PATCH taps a pencil against his music stand to indicate the sound of a telegraph.)

SALLY: Two State Department couriers were held up and robbed today by a masked gunman as they returned to their car from a service area on the New York Thruway, just outside Rochester.

(Tapping stops)

SALLY: According to official sources, they were deprived of several top secret State Department documents along with some purchases from a fast-food restaurant….

WALTER: *(To audience)* We begin a really cool tracking shot past a neon sign saying Nick's Bar. The camera goes through the front door into a crowded room where we discover the source of some piano music. It's Myrna, playing a small upright piano.

MYRNA: *(Singing)*
I'll go home and get my panties,
You go home and get your scanties,
And away we'll go…

OTHER ACTORS: *(Singing)* Mmmmm…

ALL: Off we're gonna shuffle,
Shuffle off to Buffalo…

WALTER: *(To audience)* We follow a waiter as he carries a single drink on a tray up to a door marked "private." The waiter knocks…

(All knock three times on their music stands.)

NICK: Come in.

WALTER: *(To audience)* We enter an inner office, and see a man at a desk. He is dealing a hand of solitaire to himself, briskly and efficiently.

(NICK *mimes this.)*

SWING ACTOR: *(As* TEDDY, *a waiter)* Here's your Canada Dry ginger ale, Nick.

NICK: Thanks, Teddy.

TEDDY: Sure you don't want me to add a splash of Canadian Club whiskey?

NICK: No thanks, Teddy. Much as I prefer Canadian beverages, I have no intention of falling off the wagon.

TEDDY: I hear you also prefer Canadian democracy.

NICK: I prefer any government that enables its people to live a decent life.

TEDDY: I think democracy is a delicate flower. It requires a solid economy, a humane culture, and an educated populace in order to thrive and grow.

NICK: What was your job before you came to Buffalo?

TEDDY: Professor of Economics at a state university. But I was forced out because of my articles warning against our appalling deficit.

NICK: Good luck in Canada, Teddy.

TEDDY: Thanks—if I can only get an exit visa.

WALTER: *(To audience)* There is a noisy scuffle outside the door. Smash cut to Renzo, a small, agitated man, who bursts in..

SWING ACTOR: *(Now as* RENZO*)* Nick: I've got to see you! Privately!

NICK: Come in, Renzo… Shut the door as you go, Teddy.

RENZO: Nick, I'm in trouble.

NICK: Don't tell me they're finally catching up with you for smuggling liberals across the Niagara River. You've made more money than any other coyote in Erie County.

RENZO: A man's got to live, Nick.

NICK: So what's the problem this time?

RENZO: Did you hear about those two State Department couriers who were robbed by a masked gun man on the Thruway?

NICK: It's all over town.

RENZO: I happened to be said gun man.

NICK: I suspected as much.

RENZO: Why?

NICK: I notice a large take-out bag from Burger King emerging from your pocket.

RENZO: Guess what's in it,

NICK: I see the hint of a fried onion ring.

RENZO: More than that. Look at these, Nick

NICK: What the hell are those?

RENZO: These are called Letters of Transit

NICK: Letters of what?

RENZO: Transit, Nick. Permission to travel to anywhere else in the world. Stamped with the seal of the Republican Party, and signed by you-know-who. They allow whoever carries them to leave the country without even being strip-searched. They're worth a fortune, Nick!

NICK: Congratulations.

RENZO: Yes, but the police have already narrowed the search down to me.

NICK: Yes well, you always end up as the usual suspect, Renzo.

RENZO: But if they find these on me, I'm a sure candidate for Cuba. Will you hold them for me, Nick? I don't trust anyone else.

NICK: Sorry, Renzo. It's against my religion.

RENZO: You have no religion, Nick.

NICK: Oh yes. I'm a practicing atheist.

RENZO: But aren't you capable of compromise, Nick?

NICK: Actually I am. I'm passionately opposed to junk food, but I love fried onion rings.

RENZO: It's my last one, Nick.

NICK: Give it to me, and you can leave those documents here as long as it's not overnight.

RENZO: Thanks, Nick. I'll pick them up as soon as they've searched me and found me lacking.

NICK: Then what will you do with them?

RENZO: Sell them to the richest emigre in town, and shove off for Las Vegas.

NICK: I hear Las Vegas is now the most prosperous city in the country. Rampant capitalism and addictive gambling seem to go hand in hand.

RENZO: All the more reason for me to practice my roulette. Can you tweak the wheel so I win, Nick?

NICK: I can, but I won't.

RENZO: I'm beginning to think you don't like me, Nick.

NICK: I don't like anybody, Renzo. Haven't you learned that by now?

WALTER: *(To audience)* We follow Nick as he goes down into the bar, eating the onion ring. Unobtrusively, he slips the letters of transit under the lid of the piano.

NICK: How's it going, Myrna?

MYRNA: Fine, Boss. Good crowd tonight. I'm steeping them in nostalgia by doing songs about the Erie Canal…. *(Singing)*
Low bridge… Everybody down…
Low bridge…'cause we're coming through a town…
And you'll always know your neighbor, you'll always know your pal
If you've ever navigated on the Erie Canal…

WALTER: *(To audience)* Nick is approached by Charley Washington, the local Police Chief.

CHARLEY: Nick! I've been looking for you. I just got word that a major government bigwig is coming into town.

NICK: Who this time?

CHARLEY: The Deputy Secretary for Homeland Security. He wants you to save him your best table.

NICK: Is he a Republican?

CHARLEY: What else?

NICK: Then he'll take it anyway. And tear up the tab.

CHARLEY: Go easy, Nick. I'm a Republican, too.

NICK: You're a Republican, Charley, because you've got five kids and need a job. I happen to know you voted for Kerry back in Ought Four.

CHARLEY: I wish you wouldn't bring up my youthful indiscretions.

NICK: I'm sure you'll bring up mine.

CHARLEY: Well, I did happen to glance at your F B I file recently.

NICK: Knew it.

CHARLEY: Seems you were once a major trouble-maker at Buffalo State University.

NICK: I was, wasn't I? I led a protest march for student discounts at Bills' games.

CHARLEY: Do you get anywhere?

NICK: No. The corporate interests had already commandeered all the good seats. So now I'm just a simple ole home boy, running his Daddy's bar.

CHARLEY: And making big bucks off Buffalo's booming new economy.

NICK: And dying of boredom while I'm doing it.

CHARLEY: You won't be bored tonight, Nick. I'm planning to stage a raid to impress our visiting dignitary.

NICK: Oh Christ, Charley. Does that mean I have to close down the gambling?

CHARLEY: Naw. The government encourages gambling these days. It helps pay for our war on terror.

NICK: "War on terror." You know, Charley, that expression always bothered me. How do you fight a war against an emotion?

CHARLEY: I don't know, but it gets votes, Nick.

NICK: But it's being overused. How about changing it to…let's see…"The Struggle against Stress"? … Or maybe just simply "The Battle Against the Bad."

CHARLEY: I'll bring it up with our visiting Secretary.

WALTER: *(To audience)* Cut to the Greater Buffalo International Airport as a corporate jet skids to a stop on the tarmac. Abner Patch, a Southerner in a natty suit, with one hand carrying a Bible, the other holding down his hairpiece, comes down the stair-ladder followed by his young aide, named Travis.

CHARLEY: Welcome to Buffalo, Mr. Secretary.

SECRETARY PATCH: *(Southern accent)* Thank you, Chief. I hope you folks have noticed this here Holy Bible. This is my reference material, my outside reading, and my basic operating manual. *(To his aide)* When we get to the hotel, Travis, I want it right by my bed when I pray the Lord my soul to keep.

SWING ACTOR: *(As* TRAVIS*)* Thy will be done, Mister Secretary.

CHARLEY: How fortunate you are to have avoided one of our famous Buffalo blizzards, Mister Secretary.

SECRETARY PATCH: No problem, Chief. We from the red states have learned to adjust to all sorts of climates. You can blow ill winds at us till you're blue in the face…. You might write that down, Travis.

TRAVIS: I already have, Mister Secretary.

SECRETARY PATCH: But I'm not here to discuss global warming, Chief. I hope your boys have found the man who robbed our two couriers on the Thruway.

CHARLEY: We are working on that, Mister Secretary.

SECRETARY PATCH: Work harder. I understand this city has become a hotbed of would-be exiles. In fact, I've received word that Walter Wellman and his wife have arrived here with the expressed intention of visiting Canada.

CHARLEY: Walter Wellman, the distinguished television commentator?

SECRETARY PATCH: *Erstwhile* commentator, sir. Because of his continual attacks on American policies, he has lost corporate sponsorship on both network and cable television. *(Aside to* TRAVIS*)* He occasionally gets on Charlie Rose, but Charlie interrupts him so much it doesn't make any difference.

CHARLEY: And you say he's coming to Buffalo?

SECRETARY PATCH: That's why I'm here. We must prevent Wellman from leaving the country and delivering his diatribes elsewhere. How can we possibly spread freedom around the world when this man is free to criticize it?

CHARLEY: Interesting point.

SECRETARY PATCH: I assume that he'll show up at Nick's bar, which the C I A tells me is a major hang-out for disgruntled Democrats. Have you reserved us a table?

CHARLEY: The best, sir.

SECRETARY PATCH: Then we'll go there this evening. But for now, I want a police escort to my hotel. I suddenly feel heartsick and heavy-laden.

CHARLEY: Because of Walter Wellman, sir?

SECRETARY PATCH: No. Tell him, Travis.

TRAVIS: The Secretary wants to go to the bathroom, Chief..

CHARLEY: Noted. And understood.

WALTER: *(To audience)* Cut to Nick's Bar.

MYRNA: *(Singing)*
…For the E-ri-ee was a-risin
And the gin was getting' low,

ALL: *(Joining in)*
And I scarcely think
We'll get a drink,
Till we get to Buffalo…

CHARLEY: O K, boys, Renzo is now gambling in the back room. I'll go nab him. But I want a man at every exit so he can't get away…

ALL: *(As cops)* Right, Chief.

CHARLEY: Renzo, my friend, I want you to come down to the station for a little questioning.

SWING ACTOR: *(As RENZO)* No need, Chief. You can search me right here.

CHARLEY: Put on these handcuffs, please..

RENZO: So you can make me do the perp-walk through the main lounge? Not on your life.

CHARLEY: Oh come on. Some of the most distinguished C E Os in America are wearing handcuffs these days. I hear Nieman-Marcus now offers a platinum version..

RENZO: O.K. but let me just in cash in my…

WALTER: *(To audience)* Renzo dashes from the room, and runs into Nick.

RENZO: Nick, they want to humiliate me! Help me, hide me, do something!

NICK: Sorry, Renzo.

RENZO: Nick, I'm your friend!

NICK: I have no friends. I stuck my neck out years ago, and look where it got me.

RENZO: You disappoint me, Nick!

NICK: I disappoint myself.

WALTER: *(To audience)* Renzo turns and dashes out the door. There is the sound of a major scuffle outside.

(All bang on sides of their seats.)

WALTER: And then silence. Cut to the main room of the bar where the Secretary Patch and Travis are being served drinks at a table.

CHARLEY: My apologies for the disturbance, Mister Secretary.

SECRETARY PATCH: May I assume that you were arresting a known terrorist, carrying vital government documents?

CHARLEY: We're searching him thoroughly right now, Mister Secretary.

WALTER: *(To audience)* We hear a loud yelp.

RENZO: Yelp.

SECRETARY PATCH: I must say, Chief, I'm enjoying this establishment., subversive though it may be. Would you introduce me to the proprietor?

CHARLEY: Certainly, sir.

(CHARLEY beckons to NICK, who stands up.)

SECRETARY PATCH: Sit down, sir.

NICK: I prefer to stand.

SECRETARY PATCH: What is your profession, may I ask? Besides owning a bar.

NICK: I am a recovering alcoholic.

SECRETARY PATCH: So I have heard. The Chief here provided me with resume. Show it to him, Travis.

NICK: Hey. This is all wrong. My eyes aren't blue at all

SECRETARY PATCH: I suspect everything about you is blue, sir. And disgruntled. Perhaps you could tell me what exactly gruntles you?

NICK: Sure. I think we are not now, nor have we ever been, the greatest country in the world. And it pisses me off that we strut around saying we are.

SECRETARY PATCH: Oh really?

NICK: Yes. In fact, in some ways, we're not even in the top ten.

SECRETARY PATCH: In what ways, may I ask?

NICK: Infant mortality, basic education, health care for the poor, attitude towards the environment.

SECRETARY PATCH: Stop!

NICK: There's more.

SECRETARY PATCH: Men have been sent to Guantanimo for less, sir.

NICK: All the worse.

MYRNA: *(To audience)* Nick goes, as a handsome man and a beautiful woman now enter the bar..

SALLY: This place feels dangerous, Walter. We shouldn't have come.

WALTER: We had to, Sally. We're supposed to meet a man named Renzo here. Apparently he has acquired documents which will get us into Canada.

SALLY: Don't tell me you forgot to renew our passports.

WALTER: Our applications were rejected.

SALLY: For what reason?

WALTER: They didn't say. *(As if to a waiter)* Two cognacs, please.

MYRNA: *(Singing)*
I had a mule, her name was Sal…
Fifteen miles on the Erie Canal…

WALTER: That's strange. The piano-player seems to know your name.

SALLY: I must say she looks familiar….

SWING ACTOR: *(As* MAN, *foreign accent)* Excuse me, sir. Would you like to buy some jewelry for the lady?

WALTER: No thank you.

MAN: Perhaps if you'd look, I have some lovely antique bracelets. *(To audience)* He rolls back his sleeve to reveal a row of blue bracelets running up his arm. Close-up of the inscription on the bracelet: "I voted Blue. How about you?"

WALTER: *(Low voice)* Perhaps we could do business.

MAN: Meet me over at the bar.

WALTER: Excuse me a moment, darling.

(WALTER *and* SWING ACTOR *turn their music stands to face each other, as if they were at the bar.)*

MAN: *(Furtively)* Welcome to Buffalo, Walter Wellman. We've been waiting for you.

WALTER: Are you Renzo?

MAN: No. Renzo is being renditioned.

WALTER: Renditioned?

MAN: Sent to a place where they condone torture.

WALTER: I suppose you mean Texas.

MAN: Yes, but when he was searched, they found nothing but two tickets to the Las Vegas version of *The Phantom of the Opera.*

WALTER: That's torture enough…I need to get to Canada. I'm scheduled to speak at the University of Toronto..

MAN: Maybe we can help. Come to a meeting tonight in basement of the Erie County Library.

WALTER: How do I get there?

MAN: Just tell any cabbie you want to look at the original manuscript of Mark Twain's *Huckleberry Finn*. We're all very proud of that here in Buffalo, and he'll take you there immediately.

WALTER: I hate to think what Twain would say about us today…. But we're looking suspicious… *(Louder)* Perhaps you can sell me one of those wonderful bracelets…

MYRNA: *(To audience)* Sally gets up from her table and goes to the piano-player.

SALLY: Hello, Myrna.

MYRNA: Sally.

SALLY: Play it, Myrna.

MYRNA: You shouldn't have come here, Sally.

SALLY: Play the song.

MYRNA: I've forgotten it.

SALLY: You know it cold, Myrna. Please. Play it for me.

MYRNA: *(Singing)*
They called her frivolous Sal…
A peculiar sort of a gal…
With a heart that was mellow,
An all-round good fellow,
Was my gal Sal…

NICK: Myrna! I told you I never wanted to hear that particular—

SALLY: Hello, Nick.

MYRNA: *(To audience)* There is a long pause. *(Pause)* But not too long.

NICK: What brings you here, Sally?

SALLY: The same thing that brings everyone else to Buffalo: a yearning for a better world.

NICK: Oh really? I thought you might have come to enjoy our weather.

SALLY: I see you're still angry with me, Nick.

NICK: Angry? Why should I be angry? You ruined my life, that's all.

WALTER: Sally, I think it's time we returned to our hotel.

SALLY: Nick, this is my husband Walter Wellman....

NICK: Your husband, Sally? You're married now? And to the famous Walter Wellman? I see you picked a major political activist.

WALTER: We picked each other, sir, and are delighted with the results. As one of your waiters might say, "good choice!"

SALLY: Nick here is an old acquaintance, Walter. We worked on the Al Gore campaign together, back in 2000.

WALTER: A noble enterprise. Let me shake your hand, sir.

NICK: I'll say this, Wellman. In a simpler world, we might have become friends.

WALTER: I see no reason why we still shouldn't be.

NICK: Maybe your wife can answer that.

WALTER: Oh really? Come darling, time to go. It's been a long day. And I have the sense it might be a longer night.

SECRETARY PATCH: Excuse me, folks, but I want to pay my respects to the famous Walter Wellman. Have you come to Buffalo to cause trouble, sir?

NICK: He came to see a baseball game,

SECRETARY PATCH: Buffalo has no major league baseball team.

NICK: He was misinformed.

WALTER: I'm hoping to visit Canada, Mister Secretary..

SECRETARY PATCH: I thought as much.

NICK: I should think you two might have met before in the corridors of power.

SECRETARY PATCH: We have indeed. When I was a member of the revived House Un-American Activities Committee, Mister Wellman here testified in front of us.

NICK: I assume you took the Fifth, Wellman.

SECRETARY PATCH: He did not. In fact, he told us more than we wanted to know.

WALTER: I believe I spoke the truth.

SALLY: Don't get him started, please.

SECRETARY PATCH: (To NICK) When we accused him of being a Benedict Arnold, he said he considered that a compliment.

WALTER: I did, and still do.

SALLY: That's enough, darling.

WALTER: I simply said that Arnold betrayed his country because he realized that once we had cut loose from England's traditional culture, there would be nothing to prevent us from turning into a crass, vulgar, materialistic society interested only in making money.

SALLY: O K, O K, that's enough.

SECRETARY PATCH: *(To* NICK*)* And he went on to attack Abraham Lincoln.

WALTER: I did.

SALLY: But don't do it now.

SECRETARY PATCH: He said that Lincoln never should have fought the War Between the States.

WALTER: I did….

SECRETARY PATCH: The Southern members of the committee applauded him at that point.

NICK: Jesus, Wellman.

SALLY: Let's leave it there, please.

WALTER: No, I have to explain, Sally. *(To* NICK*)* I testified that Lincoln should have let the South go. Then he should have proclaimed total Emancipation throughout the North and blockaded all Southern trade at home and abroad. They wouldn't have lasted a month. Then he should have welcomed them back only after they freed their slaves and come up with a decent program of civil rights. If he had done that, he would have saved hundreds of thousands of lives and prevented one hundred years of segregation. THAT would have made a more perfect union.

NICK: Hmmm.

SECRETARY PATCH: Yes, well, no matter. We Red States won in the end, didn't we?

WALTER: Only temporarily, I hope.

SECRETARY PATCH: These good people here might also want to know that you concluded your testimony in front of our committee by making some very disparaging remarks about American democracy and freedom.

SALLY: Will you please stop egging him on, Mister Secretary? He's his own worst enemy.

SECRETARY PATCH: At one point he said—

WALTER: I'll say it again. We're not really a democracy at all, if we ever were. We're an oligarchy, which means government by the rich, for the rich, and dedicated to the proposition that they get even richer, at the expense of everyone else.

SECRETARY PATCH: There! You see? You see why the American government cannot possibly allow this man to wander around the world, spreading such lies!

WALTER: I have one more point to make.

SALLY: No, Walter. Please! Enough's enough.

WALTER: Sorry, Sally. I'm on a roll now. In two days I am committed to make a major speech in Toronto, which I hope will be taped and televised for general consumption throughout the world. I will begin by saying that not so long ago we went to war on the basis of lie - a lie we asked for, a lie we wanted, a lie which gave us the excuse to do what we planned to do anyway. Now what does that say about a country which does this? And what does it say about a people that let it happen? I'll tell you what I say. I apologize. I apologize to the families of the kids who were killed, And to the families of the many more of the Iraqi citizens who were killed, too. I apologize for our country's appalling self-righteousness and arrogance and intrusiveness all over the world. And after I've said all that, I'll go on to suggest numerous ways we can make amends. Because when I think of the good we could do—

SWING ACTOR: (Interrupting; as TRAVIS) It's past your bed-time, Mister Secretary..

SECRETARY PATCH: You're right, Travis. But I almost forgot why I came to Buffalo in the first place. There seems to be some major difficulty with your passports, Mister Wellman. I wonder if you'd care to stop by the Homeland Security office tomorrow morning at shall-we-say ten A M?

WALTER: I'll be there.

SECRETARY PATCH: Then goodnight... Say goodnight, Travis.

TRAVIS: Good night all

SECRETARY PATCH: (As they go) You don't need to tell me a story tonight, Travis. Just unpack my jammies and my Polident. And have my Bible open at a particularly violent passage in the Old Testament.

SALLY: We should go too, Walter.

WALTER: Did I say too much?

SALLY: You always do…. Goodnight, Nick.

NICK: Sleep well, Sally. If you can.

SALLY: Oh please.

CHARLEY: *(To* NICK*)* What happened? The Secretary looked furious.

NICK: Say, Charley, do me a favor, will you? Tell your boys to clear the place out, Call it a raid or something.

CHARLEY: Really, Nick? The night is young, the joint is jumping..

NICK: Not for me it isn't. I want to be alone

WALTER: *(To audience)* The chief blows a whistle and he and his men start to remove the customers. Fade to later that night. A single light illuminates the area around the piano. Myrna improvises idly on the piano. Nick sits at a table with a bottle and a glass. He is pouring himself another drink.

MYRNA: Lay off, Boss.

NICK: My first drink in fifteen years. *(He might mime drinking here.)*

MYRNA: Make it your last, Boss.

NICK: Of all the gin joints, along the entire length of our long border with Canada, she had to walk into mine.

MYRNA: Boss, let me call A A.

NICK: I've got to see her first.

MYRNA: She's sound asleep, Boss, at the local Marriott.

NICK: I know she'll show up.

MYRNA: Maybe, but you shouldn't be here when she does. Let's take the car and drive. We'll go look at Niagara Falls. They've got colored lights on them now, and background music sung by the Mormon Tabernacle Choir.

NICK: We can have background music right here, Myrna. You played it for her, play it for me.

MYRNA: I don't want to, Boss….

NICK: Do it. Or no Christmas bonus.

WALTER: *(To audience; he might leave his music stand here and speak more intimately to the audience)* The music modulates into a lush, romantic orchestral version of *My Gal Sal* as we flashback to the summer of the year 2000. We see the storefront headquarters of the Gore-Lieberman campaign. Through the window, one can see large posters and photographs of the candidates. At the front desk a younger-looking Sally sits at a table, stuffing campaign literature into envelopes. A similarly younger Nick is walking by outside. He glances in the window, sees Sally, starts to move on, then stops and goes inside. Cut to Sally, working at the desk. She looks up as Nick approaches.

NICK: Hiya.

SALLY: May I help you?

NICK: You got a lot of envelopes to lick there.

SALLY: I know. Tomorrow I plan to bring along my Labrador retriever to help.

NICK: In four years, you won't need to do any mailings. It will all happen on the internet.

SALLY: In four years, we won't even need that. Gore will be easily reelected.

NICK: You think?

SALLY: *(As she licks envelopes)* Absolutely. Who will they get to run against him? Not Bush again, that's for sure. Did you see him last night on Brokaw?

NICK: Clueless.

SALLY: I agree.... So. You want to volunteer?

NICK: I guess.

SALLY: You guess? You walked in here, didn't you?

NICK: Yeah, but only because I saw you through the window. Want to have lunch?

SALLY: With you?

NICK: Who else?

SALLY: Now?

NICK: Whenever.

SALLY: Oh I don't know....

NICK: Come on. I'm new in town and need company.

SALLY: Where are you from?

NICK: Buffalo.

SALLY: Buffalo! All that snow!

NICK: I work in my Dad's bar up there. Which helps pay for law school at night. But I need a break, frankly. So I thought I'd just take the summer off and check out the big city. I was just walking along and saw you.

SALLY: That sounds like a Buffalo snow job.

NICK: No, it's true. How about you? You work here full-time?

SALLY: Just till election day. I work for the Nature Conservancy, but they gave me a special leave of absence to work here this summer, because Gore is so good on the environment.

NICK: So. Lunch?

SALLY: Oh hell. Why not?

WALTER: *(To audience)* The music swells into a romantic arrangement of *My Gal Sal* as we watch them go off down the street, and then settle into their seats at an outdoor café. Cut to the waiter bringing them the bill.

NICK: I've got the tab.

SALLY: Let's split it.

NICK: I invited you.

SALLY: But I'm richer than you are.

NICK: How do you know?

SALLY: I can tell.

NICK: Am I that much of a doofus?

SALLY: You seem rather refreshing, actually. I've been involved with a guy who—oh well, skip it. It's over, anyway.

NICK: O K. I'll make a deal with you. I'll pay this, and you pay for dinner.

SALLY: Dinner? O K. Why the hell not?

WALTER: *(To audience; again he might leave his stand here and move among the audience)* More music. We see the standard montage of scenes as we watch a young couple fall in love in the summer in New York. We see them at dinner, toasting each other with wine; window-shopping along Fifth Avenue; waiting in line for tickets at some movie; dancing at some club; walking Sally's Labrador and chatting with other dog owners; kissing in the back of a taxi; strolling arm in arm through Central Park.

SALLY: Don't you feel guilty?

NICK: About what?

SALLY: Goofing off this way. We haven't checked in on campaign headquarters in over week.

NICK: We're volunteers, after all.

SALLY: Still. Don't you care about politics?

NICK: I do, sort of. I just like it better when politics are not the issue.

SALLY: Do you still feel like a doofus?

NICK: Oh sure. I'm a rube from Buffalo, but I'm learning fast.

WALTER: *(To audience)* He kisses her.

(WALTER *gives* NICK *the high five.)*

WALTER: They walk by a sign saying "Shakespeare in the Park. Tonight: *All's Well That Ends Well*". We see them settling into their seats; looking at each other at the door of her apartment; waking up in bed together in the morning; cycling along the Hudson; visiting the Cloisters; Nick moving his stuff into Sally's apartment; Nick and Sally going to a bar where they go up to the piano-player—who is Myrna.

SALLY: *(To* MYRNA*)* Hi. Do you know Al Gore's campaign song?

MYRNA: Al Gore doesn't have a campaign song. That's one of his problems.

SALLY: He has no problems.

MYRNA: You wish.

SALLY: At least play Clinton's song, then. *(Sings briefly)*
"Don't stop…thinking about tomorrow…"

MYRNA: We're not supposed to get political here, lady. I could lose my job.

NICK: What's your name?

MYRNA: Myrna.

NICK: Here's my card, Myrna. My Dad owns a bar in Buffalo. If you lose your job, you can always play there.

SALLY: She might not want to play in Buffalo.

MYRNA: Actually I do. I got a sister in Buffalo.

NICK: So play what the lady wants.

MYRNA: What's the lady's name?

SALLY: Sally.

MYRNA: What if I play this? *(She plays and sings.)*
They call her frivolous Sal,
A peculiar sort of a gal…

WALTER: *(To audience)* The music continues under as we see a doorman on a street seeping up the fall leaves in front of an apartment house. Sally and Nick, now wearing fall jackets, arrive laughingly at campaign headquarters.

(SALLY *and* NICK *laugh.)*

WALTER: They are approached by a campaign worker.

SWING ACTOR: *(As* CAMPAIGN WORKER*)* Where the hell have you guys been?

SALLY: We've been falling in love.

NICK: Now we're stopping in to say goodbye.

SALLY: We're flying to Paris.

WORKER: Paris? Why?

SALLY: Why? Because it's the most romantic city in the world.

NICK: And the perfect place to plan our future.

WORKER: When do you go?

NICK: Tomorrow night.

WORKER: That's Election Day, tomorrow!

NICK: Which is why were going.

SALLY: And why they gave us a great travel package: flight over and back plus hotel accommodations on the West Bank.

NICK: You mean Left Bank, Sally.

SALLY: Sorry.

WORKER: Hey guys, know something? We could really use you here. Manning the phones. Taking old people to vote.

SALLY: Oh come on. Gore's got it made.

WORKER: Yeah? Did you see the latest poll?

NICK: Did you watch the last debate?

SALLY: Bush was…

NICK & SALLY: Hopeless.

NICK: We'll watch the returns out at Kennedy….

SALLY: And celebrate all across the Atlantic.

WORKER: I hope you're right, fellas!

NICK: How can we not be? The American people may be dumb, but they're not *that* dumb.

*(*SALLY *and* NICK *laugh.)*

WALTER: *(To audience)* They leave, laughing. Cut to Sally's bedroom. Nick is closing his suitcase. Sally is still packing her things, her dog Lucy beside her.

SALLY: Tell you what. You take a cab out to Kennedy and I'll meet you out there.

NICK: Why?

SALLY: Because I've got stuff to do: deliver Lucy to a friend, ask the Nature Conservancy for an extra week off, buy a new blouse….

NICK: I'll come with you.

SALLY: You'll just get impatient and we'd have our first fight. Now go. Maybe if you're early, they'll give you seats by the exits. Meet you in the waiting area, O K? O K. Bye-bye. Love ya.

WALTER: *(To audience)* She pushes him gently out the door.

(NICK blows her a kiss)

WALTER: Cut to the Air France waiting area at Kennedy. It's relatively empty. Nick sit, bags beside him, airline tickets in hand, watching C N N on the overhead television monitor

SWING ACTOR: *(As T V REPORTER)* Looks like Gore has taken Florida, which pretty much gives him the election.

NICK: *(Out loud, clenching his fist)* YES!

WALTER: *(To audience)* Nick looks at his watch, peers expectantly down the passageway towards where Sally should be coming from.. Cut to the television monitor.

T V REPORTER: It's beginning to look as if our Florida prediction may have been somewhat premature. Our sources now tell us the state is still up for grabs. Which means the election is still too close to call.

NICK: NO!

WALTER: *(To audience)* Nick looks again at his watch, gets up and walks down the passageway toward the security station, where there is now very little activity. He looks at his watch again, returns to his seat impatiently .

T V REPORTER: Despite Gore's sizeable majority in the country at large, we are told that if George W. Bush wins Florida's electoral votes, he may well win the election.

NICK: *(Loudly)* SHIT!

WALTER: *(To audience)* A Frenchman, also waiting for the flight, overhears him.

CHARLEY: *(As FRENCHMAN)* In France we say *"merde"*, monsieur…

SWING ACTOR: (*As* AIR FRANCE ATTENDANT*)* Air France flight number 30 for Paris now boarding, gate number fourteen.

WALTER: (*To audience*) Nick looks at his watch, grabs his bag, stands up, waits anxiously in the general area.

ATTENDANT: Last call for boarding Air France flight number 30 for Paris.

WALTER: (*To audience*) Nick is now desperate. He runs toward the security station, runs back to the Air France counter....

NICK: Any messages for me?

ATTENDANT: No, sir.

NICK: Nothing from your central office? Nothing from airport emergency?

ATTENDANT: Nothing, sir.

NICK: What'll I do?

ATTENDANT: Get on the plane, sir. The gate is closing.

NICK: I can't do that. (*Pause*) I wonder if you could apply this ticket toward another destination on another airline.

ATTENDANT: Where would you like to go, sir?

NICK: Buffalo, New York.

MYRNA: (*Singing*)
They called her frivolous Sal...

NICK: Open another bottle, Myrna.

MYRNA: Why not call it a day, Nick?

NICK: No. She'll show. She's gotta show.

(SALLY *stands up.*)

NICK: See? What did I tell you, Myrna? (*To* SALLY) Where's the spokesperson for a better America?

SALLY: He had to go to an important meeting.

NICK: Join me in a drink. For some strange reason, I feel like raising my glass and saying "Here's looking at you, kid."

SALLY: Nick, I came to explain things.

NICK: Oh? There's an explanation? Fifteen years after the fact?

SALLY: I still feel terrible about it, Nick.

NICK: What? Really? Leaving me sitting in the airport, clutching airline tickets in my hot little hand? Not even calling.

SALLY: This was back in B C remember.

NICK: B C?

SALLY: Before Cell phones..

NICK: *(To* MYRNA*)* Now she's blaming the technology.

SALLY: No, Nick. Listen. Here's what happened. Remember I told you I had leave my dog with a friend. What I didn't tell you was that friend was a man.

NICK: Oh wow. A man! How racy.

SALLY: I was living with him before I met you. I had left him because…well, because he was a Republican. And you seemed like such a breath of fresh air.

NICK: *(Sarcastically)* Gosh, Golly, Gee whiz, Sally.

SALLY: But when I dropped off Lucy, I discovered this man had changed. He had gone through a major conversion.

NICK: Oh Christ. Another born-again Republican.

SALLY: No, just the reverse. He told me he couldn't bring himself to vote for Bush so he voted for Gore. I said, "That's great, but I've got to fly to Paris with the man I love." He begged me to at least let him drive me to Kennedy.

NICK: I'll bet he drove an S U V.

SALLY: He did, but he swore he'd trade it in. So I said sure. Fine. Drive me out. I'll save a few bucks. And we piled into his car, dog and all.

NICK: Sounds ducky.

SALLY: It was, actually, until we turned on the radio. And that's when we heard about the Florida vote, and how Bush might win the election after all.

NICK: I was waiting in the airport, hearing the same story.

SALLY: My friend was totally freaked out. He pulled his car over to the side of the road. "How can you fly off to Paris?" he said, "when the future of our country hangs in the balance? Come down to Florida with me… We'll picket the polling places, monitor the recounts, and do everything we can make sure the vote is complete and fair."

NICK: This from a recent Republican?

SALLY: There's nothing like the conviction of a convert, Nick.

NICK: Yeah, yeah.

SALLY: As for me, I felt totally torn.

NICK: Oh come on.

SALLY: I did! I wanted desperately to go with you to Paris. But I also felt terribly guilty about how we goofed off over the summer. I knew that if Bush got elected, I'd be no fun at all in Paris. So I told my friend to get me to the Air France terminal so I could at least talk things over with you.

NICK: And did he?

SALLY: He tried. But the traffic was terrible. We kept leaving the highway to telephone you, which seriously slowed us down. And every public telephone booth along the way was broken. And we didn't have a cell phone. So when we finally arrived at Air France, your plane had just taken off. I checked with the attendant at the counter to see if you were on it. He said no, but that he had squeezed you onto a Jet Blue flight to Buffalo, with stops at Syracuse and Rochester.

NICK: You could have left word for me at my Dad's bar. It's is in the telephone book.

SALLY: I couldn't because my friend and I were already on the next plane to Florida.

NICK: What did you do with the dog?

SALLY: We gave her to a kindly baggage attendant.

NICK: That was big of you.

SALLY: Florida came before anything else. And when we got there, things were so hectic, and I felt so terrible about everything, that I just couldn't call. I did the same thing when I was at Wellesley, I felt so guilty about a late paper that I dropped the whole course.

NICK: I am not a course at Wellesley, Sally.

SALLY: I know that now.

MYRNA: (Singing)
They call her frivolous Sal…

SALLY: (To MYRNA) I know, I know. I'm such a jerk. (To NICK) Anyway, I threw all my energies into picketing and protesting the election, all the way to the Supreme Court.

NICK: What happened to your friend?

SALLY: Nick, I married him.

NICK: What? This guy grew up to be Walter Wellman, passionate nay-sayer to the gross excesses of a Republican administration.

SALLY: The very same..

NICK: One final question.

SALLY: Ask away.

NICK: Do you love him?

SALLY: Oh, Nick.

NICK: Do you?

SALLY: We have so much in common.

NICK: Meaning?

SALLY: Our feelings for this country. Our desire to make it better.

NICK: That's not love.

SALLY: There are many kinds of love, Nick.

NICK: That's what a prostitute said to me at the local cat house the night I got home.

(SALLY *quickly sits down.*)

MYRNA: Nice work, Boss. I suppose now you'll make me pour you another drink.

NICK: No, Myrna. Get me home instead.

MYRNA: Home? Your home is above this bar. This is where you live.

NICK: You call this living? Sometimes I wonder.

WALTER: *(To audience)* Cut to Chief's office at Buffalo Police Headquarters.

SECRETARY PATCH: Come in, come in, welcome! Chief Washington here has very kindly offered us the use of his office. Notice the pictures of distinguished Buffalonians on the walls. Grover Cleveland…Katharine Cornell…Tim Russert…

CHARLEY: Sit down, please, folks.

SECRETARY PATCH: First things first. Mister Wellman, as I suggested last night, the State Department has found certain irregularities in your passport renewals.

WALTER: Such as what, may I ask.

SECRETARY PATCH: Your unauthorized tour of Cuba. Your excursion into Iran. Your recent visit to New York.

SALLY: New York is a no-no?

SECRETARY PATCH: It soon will be, if I have anything to say about it.

WALTER: What you're saying is I can't go to Toronto and make my speech.

SECRETARY PATCH: I'm afraid not, sir.

SALLY: Do we have to stay in here in Buffalo?

SECRETARY PATCH: Not at all, dear lady. You can travel wherever you want—within the confines of the United States, of course. Or…

SALLY: Or what?

SECRETARY PATCH: I am prepared to offer you exit visas which will enable you both to travel abroad, provided you conduct yourselves simply as American tourists.

WALTER: Which means…?

SECRETARY PATCH: Which means you mill around in loud groups, take too many photographs, and gain an ungodly amount of weight.

SALLY: Knew it.

SECRETARY PATCH: You must also refuse all interviews and make no statements, either public or private, which could in any way demean our great country.

WALTER: Do you think my silence would prevent others from speaking out? More and more people are challenging our policies every day!

SECRETARY PATCH: Perhaps so, sir. But your voice, as a former Republican, carries somewhat farther.

SALLY: This is hopeless, Walter. Let's get out of here.

SECRETARY PATCH: One moment, please. I hear you've been looking to meet a seedy chap named Renzo…

WALTER: We were sorry to hear that he was arrested.

SECRETARY PATCH: The man was a thief. He stole two special letters of transit, and we suspect he left them in the hands of that man Nick, who seems to be your friend.

WALTER: My wife knew him, once upon a time.

SECRETARY PATCH: Well then perhaps your wife should ask him for those letters….

SALLY: Never!

WALTER: My wife is adamant on that subject, Mister Secretary.

SECRETARY PATCH: Maybe you could convince her otherwise.

WALTER: I know her well enough to know not to try. Come, darling. There's nothing for us here.

CHARLEY: Enjoy your stay in Buffalo then, folks. We've got a great art gallery. We've got several buildings designed by Frank Lloyd Wright. And of course there's always Niagara Falls.

WALTER: I hear the Canadian side is much more spectacular.

SECRETARY PATCH: Ah but for you, alas, that remains to be seen.

(Pause, as SALLY *and* WALTER *sit.)*

CHARLEY: Mr. Secretary: may I ask a question?

SECRETARY PATCH: Certainly.

CHARLEY: The letters of transit.

SECRETARY PATCH: What about them?

CHARLEY: Why not simply declare them invalid, like a cancelled check?

SECRETARY PATCH: What? Cancel a letter of transit? Are you serious? And you the Chief of Police for all of Erie County? Tell him, Travis

SWING ACTOR: *(As* TRAVIS*)* There are three basic assumptions on which our country stands.

SECRETARY PATCH: Name them, Travis.

TRAVIS: Gladly. First, there's the Constitution of the United States.

SECRETARY PATCH: You wouldn't make that null and void, now would you, Chief?

CHARLEY: Of course not…

TRAVIS: Second is the right of every American to own and operate a submachine gun.

SECRETARY PATCH: You're not thinking of challenging that one, are you, Charley?

CHARLEY: Wouldn't dare. I could get killed.

TRAVIS: Yes well, and finally there's the notion of one-size-fits-all, permanent letters of transit.

SECRETARY PATCH: Think of the American movies that would fall apart without that last principle.

TRAVIS: Movies such as *Casablanca*, for example? Which won three Academy Awards.

SECRETARY PATCH: You're not thinking of rewriting a major American masterpiece, are you, Chief?

CHARLEY: No sir.

SECRETARY PATCH: Then there we are.

*(*SECRETARY PATCH *and* TRAVIS *begin to sit.)*

CHARLEY: May I ask another question?

*(*SECRETARY PATCH *and* TRAVIS *stand up.)*

SECRETARY PATCH: Certainly. Go ahead.

CHARLEY: Why did you mention these letters of transit to the Wellmans?

SECRETARY PATCH: To whet their appetites.

CHARLEY: I don't understand.

SECRETARY PATCH: My dear Chief, if we can somehow engineer a situation where Wellman is caught holding those letters, you'd have reason to shoot him, wouldn't you?

CHARLEY: Shoot him?

SECRETARY PATCH: For possessing stolen property.

CHARLEY: That hardly calls for shooting.

SECRETARY PATCH: Accidentally? During a struggle? For the good of the country?

CHARLEY: I'd like to think…

SECRETARY PATCH: Chief, a man like Wellman can do tremendous harm even when contained within the confines of greater Buffalo. The only way to make the world safe for democracy is to eliminate him as soon as we can. We Americans have had to do this time and again over the years. Mossadegh in Iran, Allende in Chile. Now Wellman in Buffalo.

CHARLEY: I hope we can find another way.

SECRETARY PATCH: I hope we can't. I'm beginning to wonder about you, Chief.

CHARLEY: Why, sir?

SECRETARY PATCH: You ask foolish questions. You avoid eye contact. You keep glancing up at the photograph of Tim Russert. I'm forced to ask which side are you on?

CHARLEY: Why do there always have to be sides?

SECRETARY PATCH: Because we have a two-party system. So which one are you?

CHARLEY: I'm beginning to wonder myself.

SECRETARY PATCH: That's what I thought. I've got my eye on you, Chief. Need I say that you should arrest at least one Wellman, if not two, before my stay here is quite over.

CHARLEY: Yes sir.

SECRETARY PATCH: Now let's go visit that art gallery, Travis. Arrange for a photographer. Make sure I'm not photographed next to a nude.

CHARLEY: You object to nudity, Mister Secretary?

SECRETARY PATCH: Of course. Except when I'm visiting strip bars at the tax-payer's expense.

(SECRETARY PATCH *and* TRAVIS *sit down, laughing.*)

CHARLEY: Lots of activity here tonight, Nick.

NICK: Yeah, and know what? I wasn't sure we'd be able to open. Someone broke in this afternoon and make a mess of the place.

CHARLEY: Oh really?

NICK: It was almost as if they were searching for something.

CHARLEY: Do you think they found it?

NICK: I'm sure they didn't.

MYRNA: *(To audience)* Secretary Patch comes in with Travis. They settle at a table, noisily demanding bourbon and beer. Walter approaches Nick.

WALTER: Hello, Nick.

NICK: Where's your wife?

WALTER: She's a bit under the weather tonight. So I came to talk to you, Nick.

NICK: Talk away.

WALTER: Privately, if possible..

NICK: Sounds serious. Come to my office.

(*They turn a quick full circle.*)

WALTER: How much do you want for the Letters of Transit, Nick?

NICK: Not a thing.

WALTER: You'd give them to me free?

NICK: I won't give them to you at all.

WALTER: I'm prepared to pay a considerable amount of money.

NICK: I knew you were a radical, Wellman. I didn't know you were a rich one.

WALTER: I have very little money of my own, Nick. I am hoping that the money would come from contributions all across America..

NICK: Are you tax-deductible?

WALTER: Of course not.

NICK: Then dream on.

WALTER: Do you plan to use the letters yourself?

NICK: What? And leave Buffalo, now that the joint is jumping? Not on your life.

WALTER: Why sit on them, when they could do so much good?

NICK: Personal reasons.

WALTER: What is it with you, Nick? People tell me you used to have a strong social conscience. And then suddenly all that changed.

NICK: My Dad died, that's what changed. I had to take over his bar.

WALTER: I suspect there's another reason..

NICK: Ask your wife.

MYRNA: *(To audience)* Downstairs, Secretary Patch and Travis move toward Myrna's piano.

SECRETARY PATCH: Move over, my friend…

MYRNA: Hey!

SECRETARY PATCH: I'm taking over by eminent domain. I feel the need to tickle them ivories. *(Sings, with TRAVIS:)*

SECRETARY PATCH & TRAVIS:
Onward Christian Soldiers, marching as to war,
With the cross of Jesus going on before…

MYRNA: Walter comes in, strides to a large table of younger people, and gets them to start singing,

WALTER: *(Chanting)* Don't stop…

(SALLY joins in.)

SALLY & WALTER: Thinking About Tomorrow,

(Others join in.)

ALL: Don't stop, it'll soon be here.
It'll be better than before
Yesterday's gone, yesterday's gone.

MYRNA: *(To audience)* Secretary Patch's hymn is drowned out.

SECRETARY PATCH: Chief! Come here! This place is fast turning into a breeding ground for terrorism. Shut it down indefinitely.

CHARLEY: But on what grounds?

SECRETARY PATCH: Tell him, Travis.

TRAVIS: Um. Let's see. Disturbing the peace? Underage drinking? Cockroaches in the kitchen?

SECRETARY PATCH: Take your pick, Chief. Just do it!

CHARLEY: (Blowing his whistle) All right... All right... Place closed... Everybody out...

NICK: For Chrissake, Charley, what's going on?

CHARLEY: I have to shut you down. Possibly permanently.

NICK: What's the excuse this time?

CHARLEY: I am shocked, shocked, that vulgar language prevails in this quaint little Buffalo bistro frequented by innocent teen-agers.

SWING ACTOR: (As croupier) Your credit card maxed out at the roulette table, sir.

CHARLEY: Go fuck yourself.

MYRNA: (To audience) Fade to hotel bedroom. Sally is watching the news on T V.

WALTER: Hi.

MYRNA: (As NARRATOR) She turns off the television.

SALLY: Three more American soldiers killed today in Venezuela. Along with seventeen civilians.

WALTER: Headache gone?

SALLY: I didn't have one. I just don't like going to that place.

WALTER: Because of him?

SALLY: Myrna keeps playing that damn song.

WALTER: You asked for it.

SALLY: Once is enough.

WALTER: It's a sweet song.

SALLY: Do you think I'm frivolous, Walter?

WALTER: I think it's hard for you not to be.

SALLY: What do you mean?

WALTER: I must be a drag a good deal of the time. You must feel the need to leaven the lump.

SALLY: I'm not sure what I feel.

WALTER: That's the trouble with politics. We lose touch with our own feelings.

SALLY: Did you get the letters of transit?

WALTER: He's not giving them up.

SALLY: Why the hell not?

WALTER: He said "ask you".

SALLY: It's time he got over it.

WALTER: Have you?

SALLY: I never expected to see him again..

WALTER: And now you have?

SALLY: I feel…well, I have to say…

WALTER: What?

SALLY: He reminds me of a time when I wanted more out of life than just this.

WALTER: Speaking of "just this"…

SALLY: Where are you going?

WALTER: Out.

SALLY: Another meeting? What's the topic this time?

WALTER: Me. Apparently one of the waiters at Nick's heard Secretary Patch say they were going to arrest me.

SALLY: On what charges?

WALTER: My speeches are too incendiary.

SALLY: If they arrest you, I'll never see you again.

WALTER: That's why I've got to go to this meeting. They may be able to protect me.

SALLY: Oh Walter, you're hopeless.

WALTER: That's the one thing I'm not.

MYRNA: *(To audience)* He starts out, then stops.

WALTER: I love you very much, Sal. And I don't think you're frivolous at all.

MYRNA: *(To audience)* He goes. Sally goes to Walter's briefcase and pulls out a small gun. She leaves hurriedly. Cut to Nick's Bar. It is empty now. There is a light over one table where Nick sits going over the books with Myrna.

NICK: So, Myrna. How long can we stay closed before the creditors move in?

MYRNA: Two or three weeks.

NICK: Hell. Maybe that's a good thing.

MYRNA: Good? Why?

NICK: I'm getting sick of this joint, aren't you?

MYRNA: Not at all. I enjoy it here. Though I'd enjoy it more if you people didn't keep making me play that damn song.

NICK: I'm going up to bed.

(SALLY *stands up.*)

NICK: Well, well.

SALLY: I came up the back way.

NICK: So. What happens now?

SALLY: Walter's life is in danger. We need to get out of the country immediately.

NICK: I take it you're looking for the Letters of Transit.

SALLY: What do I have to do to get them?

NICK: You can start by letting me go to bed. By myself.

SALLY: Oh Nick, how can you be so calloused?

NICK: Me calloused? I seem to remember some poor rube from Buffalo being stood up in the Air France waiting area.

SALLY: I've explained all that.

NICK: Some explanation. I was just a fling, wasn't I? One of those summer excursions New York babes like to chat about in the changing rooms at Ralph Lauren's, as they try on the new fall fashions?

SALLY: The election got in my way, Nick!

NICK: Oh yeah? Well how do you think it feels to be replaced by a hanging chad?

SALLY: Don't you care what happens to our country? Don't you want to fight to change things?

NICK: I'm not fighting for anything except myself.

SALLY: I'll bet you didn't even vote in the last election.

NICK: Sure I did. I voted for Ralph Nader.

SALLY: Knew it! You're a coward, Nick. You're one of those people who choose not to choose. Dante would put you on the outskirts of Hell, if I remember that course from Wellesley.

NICK: Dante would be right.

SALLY: Yes well, Nick, you may not want to choose, but I'm forced to.

MYRNA: *(To audience)* He sees she is pointing a gun at him.

NICK: Bad choice.

SALLY: I want you to get the letters of transit and put them on that table, please. I'll simply take them and go.

NICK: Do you know how to use that thing, Sally? Have you ever shot a gun?

SALLY: Don't mock me, Nick. I'm at the end of my rope.

NICK: Then shoot me. Here, I'll get closer and make it easier for you. Aim here at my heart. You'd be doing me a favor.

SALLY: Oh Nick.

NICK: I knew you couldn't do it.

SALLY: That's because it's a fake gun. Walter uses it as a prop for his lecture on gun control.

MYRNA: *(To audience)* She bursts into tears. He takes her in his arms and kisses her.

SALLY: Oh Nick, if you knew how I've fought this. I never wanted to come to Buffalo.

NICK: No one ever does.

SALLY: But now I see you again, I want to give up politics. I've had enough of it to last a lifetime. It diminishes the soul, Nick.

NICK: Now you tell me.

SALLY: O K, call me frivolous Sal, I don't care. I've got to change my life.

NICK: Yeah, but how?

SALLY: By turning back the clock, Nick. Why can't we just jump on a plane and fly to Paris, the way we once planned.

NICK: What about Mister Incredible?

SALLY: Who?

NICK: The guy you're married to.

SALLY: Oh right. I can't think straight, Nick You'll have to do the thinking for both of us.

NICK: We're not in Saudi Arabia, Sally. Let's do our thinking together.

SALLY: O K, how about this? Give one of your Letters of Transit to Walter. Then he can go make his speeches in Toronto and everywhere else in the world.

NICK: But would he leave without you?

SALLY: We've got to make him. For the sake of the country.

NICK: That still leaves one Letter of Transit underemployed.

SALLY: Exactly. And I could use that to fly to Paris.

NICK: Where does that leave me? Once more abandoned at another airport?

SALLY: No, Nick, no. I want you to come with me. I need the letter of transit because my passport's no good. But yours must be perfectly valid.

NICK: I don't like to use it.

SALLY: Why not?

NICK: My passport photo sucks.

SALLY: Oh stop.

NICK: O K, O K. But I'm finding it kind of hard to commit here.

SALLY: I'm noticing that.

NICK: Once burned, twice shy, if you know what I mean

MYRNA: *(To audience)* There's a noise downstairs in the bar. Nick looks down. He sees Myrna helping Walter to the bar, pouring him a drink.

SALLY: What's going on?

NICK: Sssshhh. Wait here .

MYRNA: *(To audience)* Nick goes down into the bar.

NICK: What's the story, fellas?

MYRNA: Walter here was roughed up on Delaware Avenue by a bunch of angry Evangelicals coming back from a prayer meeting.

WALTER: I turned the other cheek and look where it got me.

MYRNA: So he came here, and I'm giving him a quick belt to calm his nerves.

NICK: Myrna, may I speak to you privately? *(Low to MYRNA)* I've got a guest in my room. Drive her home, will you?

MYRNA: Yes, Boss.

NICK: *(To WALTER)* What were you doing out so late?

WALTER: Returning from a meeting. It was supposed to be about me. But I managed to shift the subject to how we might keep Social Security out of the clutches of Wall Street.

NICK: Christ, man. Why bother? Fighting the same old battles, year after year? Don't you get bored?

WALTER: "Eternal vigilance", my man. Somebody's got to keep watch.

NICK: Yeah? Well, I'm glad it's not me.

WALTER: I wonder. Still waters run deep. I know that underneath your cynical exterior, you have strong feelings about a number of issues.

NICK: Name one.

WALTER: My wife.

NICK: Mmm.

WALTER: I could tell immediately, that first night we walked in here. And I could also tell something else.

NICK: What was that?

WALTER: She felt the same way about you.

NICK: Not a chance.

WALTER: She's a good woman, Nick. She's stuck by me, through some tough times. She deserves a break. Know what I wish you'd do?

NICK: Leave her alone. Right?

WALTER: Wrong. Get her out of here.

NICK: Are you serious?

WALTER: I am. Use those Letters of Transport. Take her on a trip. She's always liked Paris. That was the plan, wasn't it, a while back?

NICK: Have you been bugging my office?

WALTER: Not at all, Nick. I just thought it up. But do it, man. I love her, I'll miss her, but maybe she'll come back to me on her own terms. Frankly I'm kind of hoping you won't sleep with her, Nick, but of course that's her choice.

NICK: Are you nuts?

WALTER: No, but I'm a feminist at heart, Nick. I want to give Sally the chance to develop her own talents. For example, right now she's a lousy cook. Maybe when she gets to Paris, you could get her to enroll in one of those Cordon Bleu cooking schools, so that when she comes back, she can finally produce a good meal.

NICK: What'll you do while we're gone? Hang around Buffalo?

WALTER: Sure. Why not? Politics starts at the local level. I'll be a consultant.

NICK: You're weird, Wellman. Anyone ever tell you that?

SECRETARY PATCH: *(To audience)* Charley rushes in, followed by a couple of cops, with their guns drawn.

CHARLEY: Walter Wellman, you are under arrest.

WALTER: On what grounds?

CHARLEY: Brawling in Buffalo on a school night… Take him away… Sorry to disturb you, Rick.

NICK: You not only disturb me, you disappoint me, Charley.

CHARLEY: In what way?

NICK: Some arrest! Even a Republican judge couldn't keep the guy locked up on flimsy charges like that. He'll be out and around by noon tomorrow.

CHARLEY: We do what we can.

NICK: We can do better, Charley. Get him to come to my office tomorrow afternoon and I'll give him the letters of transit.

CHARLEY: Ah hah! I knew you had them!

NICK: I do, and when I hand them to Wellman, you can arrest him for possessing stolen goods. That should keep him in the clinker for a good long time. And get you in good with the Deputy Secretary.

CHARLEY: I'm not sure I trust you, Nick. This doesn't feel like you, somehow.

NICK: I'll give you my motive, Charley. I want Wellman out of the picture so I can reconnect with his wife.

CHARLEY: You've known her before?

NICK: There's no flame like an old flame, pal.

CHARLEY: She's very beautiful, I'll say that.

NICK: I've been saying that to myself for much too long. Now I want to say it to her, in Paris, where those letters of transit will take us. Is it a deal, Charley? I give you weirdo Wellman. You give me frivolous Sal.

CHARLEY: It's worth a try.

NICK: Good. So release him tonight, and persuade him to show up at my place tomorrow afternoon. You come too, beforehand.

WALTER: *(To audience)* Cut to the next day. Early afternoon. Exterior of Nick's bar. A sign is plastered across the front door: "Closed until further notice." Cut to the interior, now looking empty and forlorn.. Nick reaches into the back of the piano, takes out the Letters of Transit. They look important and official. A knock on the door.

(All knock on music stands.)

NICK: Come in... Ah Charley, you're right on time. Look what the cat dragged in!

CHARLEY: Those are them?

NICK: These are *they*, Charley. They're important enough to deserve good grammar.

CHARLEY: Where did you keep them, Rick? We searched the place high and low.

NICK: They were in Myrna's piano.

CHARLEY: I knew I should have kept up my music lessons.

NICK: Listen. I hear the Wellman's cab. Where do you want to hide? In a closet or under a table?

CHARLEY: I intend to preserve the dignity of my office. I'll hide in the lady's room...

SALLY: Nick, I've got to speak to you.

NICK: Where's Wellman?

SALLY: Arguing with the cabbie about the tip. He can be a terrible tightwad. But Nick, he's got things all wrong. He thinks he and I are leaving together.

NICK: Don't worry

SALLY: I am worried, Nick. You're putting me in a very tricky position!

NICK: Trust me, Sally. Trust. Here he comes.... Wellman, my man. I have a Christmas present for you.

WALTER: That feels strangely inappropriate, Nick. Seeing as how it's not Christmas, and I'm half Jewish.

NICK: Just look at these documents and you'll be singing *Joy to the World.*

WALTER: The Letters of Transit!

NICK: Exactly, man. Just fill in your names and think up a password.

WALTER: Nick, how can I ever—

CHARLEY: Walter Wellman. You are under arrest for the possession of stolen government property.

WALTER: What?

CHARLEY: And please don't try to escape, or I'll have to shoot you.

SALLY: Oh no!

CHARLEY: Come with me, Mister Wellman… And thank you, Nick.

NICK: Not so fast there, Charley.

MYRNA: *(To audience)* Nicks points a gun at Charley.

NICK: Walter, hold onto to those letters. Tight.

CHARLEY: I don't understand.

NICK: Do you have a cell phone, Charley?

CHARLEY: Doesn't everyone these days?

NICK: I want you to call the Canadian border police. I'm sure you know the number.

(CHARLEY *mimes dialing.)*

NICK: *(To others)* Notice how he dials with his thumb. I wish I could do that.

CHARLEY: It's ringing, Nick.

NICK: Tell the Canadians that Mr and Mrs Walter Wellman will be entering Canada by way of the Peace Bridge on official Letters of Transit, and you want no hassle whatsoever.

CHARLEY: *(On phone)* Hello? This is Chief Charley Washington of Homeland Security…

MYRNA: *(To audience)* Cut to Secretary Patch's hotel room. We see him answering the phone. We also see that he is in bed with Travis. And we notice his hairpiece on the night table beside him.

SECRETARY PATCH: Who is this?

CHARLEY: …William Wellman will be coming through….

SECRETARY PATCH: Something's wrong, Travis. Grab your coat and get your hat.

TRAVIS: We don't have hats.

SECRETARY PATCH: Never mind. We're going to the Peace Bridge.

CHARLEY: *(To* NICK*)* Done.

NICK: *(With gun)* Let's go. Myrna's got my car out back.

MYRNA: *(To audience)* Cut to Secretary Patch and Travis, in overcoats and little else, rushing down the corridor.

SECRETARY PATCH: Wait! We've got to go back! I forgot my hair!

TRAVIS: We'll be too late!

SECRETARY PATCH: But I can't go out looking like this!

MYRNA: *(To audience)* We see a family is coming down the corridor the opposite way. It includes a teen-ager with a Red Sox baseball cap on backwards.

TRAVIS: Mister Secretary, are you a Yankees fan?

SECRETARY PATCH: Yankees? Never!

TRAVIS: Good.

MYRNA: *(To audience)* He grabs the hat off the teenager and jams it onto the Secretary's head

TRAVIS: Sorry, kid, but this involves the security of the United States of America!

MYRNA: *(To audience)* They hurry on down the hall.

ALL: *(Standing, narrating in unison, with synchronized gestures)*
CUT! ...to the interior of Nick's car. Myrna is driving. Nick is in the front seat, turned toward the back seat, holding the gun on Charley. Sally and Walter sit side by side, anxiously looking out.
CUT! ...to the interior of the Secretary Patch's car. He and Travis sit side by side. The driver is honking frantically, trying to steer through traffic
CUT! ...to a sign saying "Peace Bridge to Canada".
CUT! ...to the approach to the bridge where long lines of cars fan out as they wait to go through a row of toll booths. Nick's car pulls over to one side, right behind another car with Canadian plates. Nick and his passengers get out of the car.

NICK: *(To SALLY and WALTER)* ...And here we are.

WALTER: Ah yes. This bridge symbolizes peace and commerce between nations.

NICK: See that Honda Hybrid parked right ahead of us? The driver is an old pal of mine from Canada. He used to sell me illegal Fourth of July firecrackers when I was more patriotic. He'll drive you right on through to Toronto, with one quick stop for duty free liquor.

WALTER: Thanks, Nick. But look at all those lines of cars ahead of us. I suppose they're all Americans, leaving our sick, sad country for a better life elsewhere.

NICK: Some are. But you'll notice there are also lots of Canadian license plates. They come over to shop now that their dollar goes so much farther than ours.

WALTER: I weep for our ruined economy.

NICK: Jump in that car, and weep there. Those Letters of Transit will allow you to drive straight through.

SALLY: Nick, I've got to speak to you.

NICK: Here, Wellman. Keep this gun on Chief Washington while I speak privately with your wife.

WALTER: My pleasure.

SALLY: *(In a low voice)* I thought we were going to Paris together, Nick.

NICK: You were misinformed.

SALLY: Oh stop it, Nick. I don't think I can take it any more—being a wife in the world of politics. Sitting on some shaky podium, perched on a folding chair, knees locked together, blinking adoringly at him as he delivers the same old boring speech. Call me frivolous or not, I can't do it any more, Nick.

NICK: You've got to, Sally. Wellman needs you at his side. You're his control and his corrective. I hate to say this, but without you to keep him in line he'd be a complete ass-hole.

SALLY: You think?

NICK: I do. And I'll tell you something else: if this what we're doing has any meaning at all, it's been about our neglect of our political responsibilities in the past. We should repair the damage by being more active in the future.

SALLY: Will you become active, too, Nick?

NICK: I'll try, Sally. Which is not to say I'll neglect my personal life. In fact, whenever you and Wellman get to Paris, I hope you'll give me a call because I'll come right over.

SALLY: Oh Nick…

NICK: I will, Sally, even if it means crossing the whole Atlantic ocean in the back of the plane. Because when I arrive, I'm seriously hoping we can arrange what the French call a *ménage a trois.*

SALLY: I'm not sure I can live with that, Nick.

NICK: Think about it, Sally. Remember that we'll be in France, and to the French, what three little people do with their personal lives doesn't amount to a hill of beans.

SALLY: Oh. Nick, you've become so sophisticated as you approach middle age.

NICK: I hope so, Sally. At least I'm a different guy from that Buffalo bozo you left waiting at the airport back when the Republicans stole the election in Florida. Now go hold the gun on the Chief of Police, while I have a short scene with your husband.

WALTER: You wanted to speak to me, Nick?

NICK: I did, and do, Wellman. I think you should know that your wife came to my room last night, looking for those letters of transit. I tried to use them as a way of getting it on with her. Well sir, she wouldn't even let me get to second base. She loves you, Wellman, though I'm not sure why. They say that love is blind, but I'm beginning to think it's stupid, too.

WALTER: I feel your pain, Nick.

NICK: One other thing, Wellman, and then I'll let you go.

WALTER: Shoot.

NICK: Do you see yourself as a permanent exile or do you plan to return some time to our godforsaken land?

WALTER: The latter, Nick. We're a shitty country these days, but I doubt if I'd really be happier anywhere else.

NICK: That's the problem, isn't it? For all of us. Now get in that car before I make more moves on your wife.

SALLY: (To audience) Sally hands the gun back to Nick, then takes Walter's arm.

WALTER: (To audience) They walk bravely to the waiting car. They get in and drive toward the one toll-booth which has an "E-Z Pass Only" on a sign above it. We see the barrier arm raise, and the car go through.

SALLY: (To audience) Cut to Secretary Patch's stretch-limo skidding to a stop. The Secretary and Travis jump out of the car.

SECRETARY PATCH: What's going on here?

CHARLEY: See that green hybrid vehicle with Canadian plates going through E-Z Pass?

SECRETARY PATCH: I do indeed.

CHARLEY: Walter Wellman and his wife are in it, and well on their way to Canada.

SECRETARY PATCH: I'll make sure that they're stopped cold on the other side.

SALLY: (To audience) The Secretary pulls out his cell phone.

SECRETARY PATCH: Give me Canadian customs immediately!

NICK: Cancel that call, Mister Secretary!

SECRETARY PATCH: Try and stop me.

WALTER: (To audience) A sudden gust of wind in this open area…

(All make wind sound.)

WALTER: …blows off the Secretary's baseball hat, revealing his bald head.

(Wind sound stops.)

WALTER: Nick quickly reaches into his pocket.

SECRETARY PATCH: Are you pulling a gun on me?

NICK: I am not. This happens to be a cell phone with a camera. Want to see your picture?

SECRETARY PATCH: Good God! I look like a silly old poof.

NICK: You sure do. And a flasher to boot, with that open overcoat.

SECRETARY PATCH: Can you see my pee-pee. Travis?

TRAVIS: What there is of it, sir.

NICK: This photograph goes onto the internet immediately unless you cancel that call, Mister Secretary...

SECRETARY PATCH: *(Quickly; into his cell phone)* Never mind, Customs. Wrong number. *(To* NICK*)* That photo could ruin my political career.

TRAVIS: All the more reason to seize the hour, sir.

SECRETARY PATCH: Explain yourself, boy.

TRAVIS: We're here, Canada is there...

SECRETARY PATCH: You're suggesting...?

TRAVIS: Marriage, sir. Provided we work out a reasonable pre-nup in the car on the way over.

SECRETARY PATCH: Meaning?

TRAVIS: Meaning you assist my career, and we take turns cooking.

SECRETARY PATCH: Could we honeymoon at Niagara Falls?

TRAVIS: I don't see any reason why not.

SECRETARY PATCH: Do I dare? Do I dare?

TRAVIS: Nixon risked relations with China, sir, and went on to be reelected.

SECRETARY PATCH: You are right, Travis. *(To* NICK*)* I am about to do something very dangerous and very brave. I'm sure we'll be roundly reprimanded by my conservative colleagues back in Washington. *(To* TRAVIS*)* But we'll always have Buffalo.

NICK: Get going, guys.

MYRNA: *(To audience)* Secretary Patch and Travis get into their limousine and head for the toll booth. The Chief comes up to Nick.

CHARLEY: You look worried, Nick.

NICK: I'm trying to figure out my next step. As far as Myrna is concerned, I'm giving her the bar. She wants it and she'll take it as long as she can play more contemporary music.

CHARLEY: What about me, Nick? You've pretty well messed me up as the local Chief of Police. .

NICK: See that fog beginning to roll in from Lake Erie, Chief.

CHARLEY: I do.

NICK: Suppose we walk off together into that… It will remind us of the confusion and ambiguity which pervades so much of contemporary life.

CHARLEY: I can't just walk away from my family.

NICK: O K. then let me think. I've said more than once that I'm a confirmed atheist. This means I don't believe in a heaven after death. But it also implies that we should work to create a better life on earth while we are still alive.

CHARLEY: In Buffalo?

NICK: And everywhere else in the world.

MYRNA: *(To audience)* Charley takes Nick's arm and they start walking into the fog.

CHARLEY: You still look worried, Nick. Do you fear for our country?

NICK: I do, but that's not why I'm worried.

CHARLEY: Are you concerned that you've messed up your personal life?

NICK: I am. But that's not it either.

CHARLEY: What is it, then, man? Your secret will be safe with me.

NICK: I can't for the life of me think of a good exit line.

CHARLEY: Nobody's perfect, Nick.

MYRNA: *(To audience)* And they disappear into the fog.

ALL: *(To audience)* The end.

END OF PLAY

www.ingramcontent.com/pod-product-compliance
Lightning Source LLC
Chambersburg PA
CBHW061057090426
42742CB00002B/77